D0611493

Faith
Will See
You Through

Edited by
Douglas Pagels

Blue Mountain Press™
Boulder, Colorado

We gratefully acknowledge the permission granted by the following authors, publishers, and authors' representatives to reprint poems or excerpts from their publications: Hazelden Foundation, Center City, MN, for "When you wonder what is coming…" and "Problems arise…" from GRATITUDE: CONFIRMING THE GOOD THINGS IN LIFE by Melody Beattie. Copyright © 1992 by Hazelden Foundation. All rights reserved. HarperCollins Publishers for "Everything starts with God" and "I pray every day…" from LADIES FIRST by Queen Latifah. Copyright © 1999 by Queen Latifah, Inc. All rights reserved. And for "I think one of the most important…" by F. Murray Abraham and "I believe that spirituality…" by Ben Vereen from QUIET TRIUMPHS by Mary Alice Williams. Copyright © 1999 by Mary Alice Williams. All rights reserved. Warner Faith, a division of Hachette Book Group, for "Everything that we receive…" and "God is not in a building…" from STARTING YOUR DAY RIGHT by Joyce Meyer. Copyright © 2003 by Joyce Meyer. Reprinted by permission of Warner Faith. All rights reserved. Faith Words, a division of Hachette Book Group, for "God's gifts are given with grace…" from KNIT TOGETHER by Debbie Macomber. Copyright © 2007 by Debbie Macomber, Inc. Reprinted by permission of Faith Words. All rights reserved. And for "God wants you to…" from YOUR BEST LIFE NOW by Joel Osteen. Copyright © 2004 by Joel Osteen. Reprinted by permission of Faith Words. All rights reserved. And for "Walking with faith is…" from WALKING IN YOUR OWN SHOES by Robert A. Schuller. Copyright © 2007 by Robert A. Schuller. Reprinted by permission of Faith Words. All rights reserved. And for "Faith really is amazing…" and "We all need to do…" from THE SECRET TO TRUE HAPPINESS by Joyce Meyer. Copyright © 2008 by Joyce Meyer. Reprinted by permission of Faith Words. All rights reserved. Tyndale House Publishers, Inc., for "Relax…," "We are the recipients," "We all mess up…," and "The present chaos…" from TO FLY AGAIN by Gracia Burnham. Copyright © 2005 by Gracia Burnham. All rights reserved. And for "When we pray persistently…" and "I have learned that…" from DON'T BET AGAINST ME! by Deanna Favre. Copyright © 2007 by Deanna Favre. All rights reserved.

Acknowledgments are continued on the last page.

Library of Congress Control Number: 2010905852
ISBN: 978-1-59842-527-7

▌▌and Blue Mountain Press are registered in U.S. Patent and Trademark Office.
Certain trademarks are used under license.

Printed in China.
First Printing: 2010

✺ This book is printed on recycled paper.

This book is printed on paper that has been specially produced to be acid free (neutral pH) and contains no groundwood or unbleached pulp. It conforms with the requirements of the American National Standards Institute, Inc., so as to ensure that this book will last and be enjoyed by future generations.

Blue Mountain Arts, Inc.
P.O. Box 4549, Boulder, Colorado 80306

Contents

(Authors listed in order of first appearance)

When you wonder what is coming, tell yourself the best is coming, the very best life and love have to offer, the best God and His universe have to send. Then open your hands to receive it. Claim it, and it is yours.

✦ Melody Beattie

Everything starts with God.

✦ Queen Latifah

Everything that we receive from God comes by faith.

✦ Joyce Meyer

Faith Will See You Through

*A*lways remember...

God will be there for you, to walk alongside you, to listen to any prayers you want to share, and to light your way if you ever get lost.

Have faith that you can make the most of each day, faith that the blessings you need will come your way, and faith that, yes... you will see your way through.

God will always be
there for you.

✧ Douglas Pagels

A New Beginning

$\mathcal{R}$elax: This is not going to be one of those glib and superficial pep talks that says, "Just praise the Lord, and all your problems will melt away!" When life spins out of control, it takes more than a few magic words to stabilize the situation.

If we truly believe that God is real, however — that He is good-hearted and loving and mindful of our trial — those facts endure apart from what we are going through. Whether the sun is shining on our circumstances or not, whether everybody likes us or hates us, whether we have plenty of food and money or none at all — God is still God. He never changes.

✧ Gracia Burnham

No matter where you go or what you do, God is there and by faith you can reach out to Him.

✦ Billy Graham

We are in the hands of a loving, compassionate, caring God. And ultimately nothing will happen to us that God cannot handle.

✦ Desmond Tutu

Since God will be my end,
Let Him be my beginning,
So that I may now fully live.

✦ Angelus Silesius

Grace and Serenity

God's gifts are given with grace; no hidden strings, no extra-duty list we have to check off. God's grace is free. God's blessings are free. We just have to accept them.

✧ Debbie Macomber

In the well-known "Serenity Prayer," we ask God to give us the serenity to accept what we cannot change; the courage to change what we can; and the wisdom to know the difference. This prayer gives us a way of integrating trustful surrender and responsible striving. We place all our trust in God, our eternal Rock, by accepting peacefully whatever we cannot change. We build our lives on the sturdy foundation of rock by having the courage and responsibility to change what we can.

✧ Wilkie Au

You can draw a line from every great success back to some rock-solid foundation. A parent. A teacher. A coach. A role model. It all starts somewhere. And for me, that somewhere is with God. I'm not here to tell other folks what to believe, but I'll tell you what I believe, and this is what works for me. It's why I'm setting these thoughts to paper right now. It's why I'm here — by the grace of God.

✧ Denzel Washington

I've come to trust in God's grace. Now I know it's there for me with the same certainty that I know there are stars in the sky.

✧ Barbara Bartocci

*W*hether or not it is clear to you, no doubt the universe is unfolding as it should. Therefore be at peace with God, whatever you conceive Him to be.

✧ Max Ehrmann

*T*he gifts I wish to give you
are my deepest love,
the safety of truth,
the wisdom of the universe
and the reality of God.

✧ Emmanuel (Pat Rodegast)

*F*aith is not as complicated as I have sometimes made it. It is not hard. Quite simply, faith is a gift, and this gift is mine for the taking.

✧ Marilyn Meberg

Unwrap the Present

God wants you to accomplish great things in life. He wants you to leave your mark on the world. He's put incredible potential, gifts, and talents within you, ready for use as you start seeing yourself as God sees you, stepping out in faith and acting on the dreams that He's placed in your heart.... Keep going; keep growing. God has much more in store for you!

✧ Joel Osteen

Life's road is rough, but you can make it; hold out your hand, and God will take it.

✧ Lon Woodrum

Traveling Together

I would rather walk with God in the dark than go alone in the light.

✧ Mary Gardiner Brainard

*I*f we're going to be able to handle life when it doesn't seem to make sense, we have to get real. We have to set our faces in the right direction and keep walking as He walked. At times the road will be long and dark, the mountains unscalable. Because we're human we won't always make the perfect choices. Sometimes it will seem we take two steps forward and one step back, but it doesn't really matter. *All that matters is being on the right road.*

✧ Sheila Walsh

I may not know where my life is going,
but I have been able to slow down enough
to understand that God and I are going there
together, that life is proceeding as it always
does, one day at a time and that if I am
willing to live at that pace, then all will be
well with me.

✧ Julia Cameron

*W*hatever your present station in life, whatever
you are called to do, wherever you are called to
go, enjoy the journey. Don't waste one day of
the precious life God has given you.

✧ Joyce Meyer

*W*alking with faith is a process of beginning
where you are with what you have, taking
small steps that have the potential for
becoming large steps.

✧ Robert A. Schuller

Prayer Is Just the Ticket

*T*o walk with God, we must make it a practice to talk with God.

✧ Joni Eareckson Tada

*Y*ears ago I fell into the habit of sharing everything that concerns me with God. I wanted to keep in touch with the one who created me and is letting me take the marvelous trip — life! Just to thank and praise Him for it makes me more aware of its wonders; and to pour out problems, frustrations, and longings to Him gives me release, reassurance, and guidance....

We do get help as we pray. Not only courage, comfort, and strength, but new understanding. There is a great deal of self-analysis in prayer, especially if we're honest and confess our faults. I think God uses this process to make us realize truths about ourselves and others; He gives us new insights for resolving problems.

✧ Marjorie Holmes

When we pray persistently, God asks us to trust Him to know what we need and when we need it. Sometimes He answers, "No." Sometimes He answers, "Wait." Sometimes He answers, "Yes."

Sometimes as we pray, we are the ones who are changed. As we draw closer to God, our desires and priorities shift — and those changes in us may be the answer to someone else's prayers, or even our own.

So whether you pray silently or loudly, don't be afraid to express your deepest feelings to God.

He loves you and wants to be close to you.

He is not unfeeling, and He is willing to forgive.

He is not afraid of your feelings or surprised by your questions.

He is not too far away to hear.

And He will answer you.

◆ Deanna Favre

Keep God in Your Heart

I wish I could tell each and every one of you that you'll achieve greatness in whatever you do. Let me be the first to tell you — you may not. But you can achieve happiness and a rich life by taking your time, keeping it simple, and getting down on your knees every once in a while to thank God for what you have and to ask Him for the faith, love, guidance, and humility we all need to get through this life.

✧ Maria Shriver

I've been knocked down, had to reach for the hand of God, dusted myself off, and gotten back up again. During these times, I've had only Him to rely on for guidance and for coping with the complex and varied challenges of motherhood — spiritually, emotionally, financially, physically.... God has taught me to hold my head high. I'm on my knees in praise every morning and every night. God is great.

✧ Janine Turner

$\mathcal{P}$rayer should be a lifestyle, not an event.

✦ Ron Mehl

$\mathcal{I}$ have a neighbor who keeps a yard and beautiful gardens, and it's by watching Harriet that I've discovered the secret to gardens: hard work....

While our relationship with God is suffused with grace, it also takes a lot of hard work.

Plain and simple, there's nothing better than daily prayer. It's hard to get in the habit, I know, and easy to get out of it. My daily life is rushed and filled with important tasks. It can seem almost impossible to pray every single day for even fifteen minutes. But if I'm honest with myself, I realize how much time I devote to television, the Internet, and all the other wonderful distractions of modern life. Surely I can cut back just a bit and give that time to God.

The result, I think, is a garden like Harriet's — lush, beautiful, and sustaining.

✦ Karen Stroup

*I*t's amazing to see what God can do through us when we just show up.

✦ Michelle Akers

I pray every day, but I don't go to God asking for a million things like, "Lord, let me hit the lottery" or "God, please let me sell a million albums." It's not about that. When I speak to God, it's a release of my soul. Some mornings, I will lie in my bed and just start talking to God as if He were in the room with me — and of course, He is.

When I am alone in nature, in my tub, or in my bed waking up in the morning, that's my time with God, when I have my personal conversation with Him. And He answers me, through other people, through events. I have faith that God exists, and I never question it. It is one of the few guarantees in my life.

✦ Queen Latifah

It's Up to You

*P*eople... might not realize just how close God is to each of us, and how much help is available if we only seek it.

✧ Marjorie Holmes

I assure you that you will make the great discovery that for your every problem, FAITH IS THE ANSWER.

✧ Norman Vincent Peale

*R*emember, it's your choice. You are as close to God as you choose to be.

✧ Rick Warren

*W*hat wings are to a bird, and sails to a ship, so is prayer to the soul.

✧ Corrie ten Boom

Spiritual Journeys

*S*o what is the soul? It is the deepest aspect of ourselves, the spiritual part that cries out for heaven, that is made to be a dwelling place for God.

✦ Sheila Walsh

I think one of the most important things is the soul and the existence of the soul and the care of the soul. When you get away from it, which I did and still do from time to time as a human being, you lose track of the reason why special things take place.

Part of our obligation in this life is to find out as much about ourselves and our place in this world as we can. That is a spiritual search.

✦ F. Murray Abraham

To me, there's no question that there's a higher power. Having faith in yourself — and in something bigger than yourself — can be crucial. Faith and spirituality are an essential part of who we are. Before everything good happened for me, I was in the very gradual process of getting spiritually correct. It continues to be an ongoing project. I firmly believe that the more spiritually correct you can be, the better off you'll be.

✦ Taylor Hicks

I believe that spirituality is the key to survival. If you can find a way to both hold on to spirituality and make it a priority in your life, then you will be "walking in the light."

✦ Ben Vereen

We are the recipients of a spiritual survival kit that includes everything we require. Whatever the threat or complication, we have what we need to cope. It's not miles away on a distant shelf, or in a pharmacy; it is already within us, just waiting to be opened and put to use.

I know that we often don't feel equipped. We look at the challenges in our life and think we are empty-handed. But we are not....

We travel through life with the survival kit of God's grace.

✦ Gracia Burnham

I have faith in God's plan for me and I know that plan is in His hands. As long as I do what I'm supposed to do to walk in His light, everything is going to be all right.

✦ Gladys Knight

God Has a Plan for Each of Us

God has a plan for each of us. And I have a feeling that there is such a wonderful plan for you!

I pray that the paths you walk and the roads you travel will take you to amazing places. Places where you see the possibilities, where you discover what it's like when dreams come true, and where you come to understand the promise and the potential of all the wonderful qualities inside you.

I pray that God's plan for you will gradually unfold before your eyes, and that — like guiding lights continually showing the way — you will find glimmers of hope and happiness shining every single day.

I pray that the people in your life appreciate what it's like to be in the presence of someone as special as you are. You have the kind of gifts that are given to so few.

God has a plan for each of us... and I think there is an especially wonderful one... for you.

✦ Douglas Pagels

Rising Above

One of the most exciting aspects of our spiritual walk is to realize that God has a plan for each of His children. He has not left us to wander in the darkness of indecision.

✦ Stan Toler

Do you get anxious at sunrise because all you can see is the tiny rim of the sun? No, because you know that if you wait long enough you will see the sun in all its brilliance. The same is true of God's plan for your life. You will never see everything in advance; but if you wait long enough, God always reveals His will.

✦ Ray Pritchard

No matter how dark, disturbing, painful, and upsetting our circumstances may seem, there is a place of peace God has for each of us as a shelter from the storm. And we can depend on Him to take us there when we look to Him for refuge.

One of the best illustrations of this is whenever we take off in an airplane on a gray, dreary, rainy day. It's amazing how we can fly right up through the dark, wet clouds — so thick that we can't see one thing out the window — and then suddenly we rise above it all and have the ability to see for miles. Up there the sky is sunny, clear, and blue. I keep forgetting that no matter how bad the weather gets, it's possible to rise above the dark and gloom of the storm to a place where everything is fine.

Our spiritual and emotional lives are similar to that. When the dark clouds of trial, struggle, grief, or suffering roll in and settle on us so thick that we can barely see ahead of us, it's easy to forget that there is a place of calm, light, clarity, and peace we can rise to. If we take God's hand in those difficult times, He will lift us up.

✦ Stormie Omartian

We all mess up. We all fall down. We all self-destruct at times. And we all need to open up and receive the warm, restoring grace that originates with our loving Lord.

✦ Gracia Burnham

Problems arise. Problems get solved. Wants and needs come into awareness. Wants and needs get met. Dreams are born. Dreams are reached. Things happen. Good things happen. Then, more problems arise. But it's all okay.

Be patient. Trust in God's timing. Don't take an item off the list just because you didn't achieve or receive something when you thought you should have....

Things happen when the time is right — when we're ready, when God is ready, when the world is ready.

✦ Melody Beattie

It's All Okay

Sometimes we use problem-solving skills that seem sensible to us, and in so doing we may see our circumstances change for the better. When that happens, we sigh with relief that yet another crisis has been averted. We may even feel pleased that we managed the crisis on our own and didn't have to bother God with it. He has enough problems without our becoming a continual burden to Him. Surely, we think He means for us to figure out a few things on our own.

But what if we *can't* figure these things out on our own? What if, at our wits' end, we feel lost in pain, confusion, desperation, and fear?...

The good news is, when our backs are against the wall — when we cry out to the Lord — He is there. God is always at our wits' end. How do we know? Because God is wherever we are. His promise is to never, ever leave us. Wherever we may wander, in foolishness or fear, God does not leave us.

✧ Marilyn Meberg

$\mathcal{L}$ord, what a joy that we may come to You with all our troubles. We cannot find peace by ourselves. Thank You that You are willing to listen and that Your telephone line is never "busy."

✦ Corrie ten Boom

$\mathcal{I}$'ve been a frequent caller on God's 911 hotline, but He has always answered, and for that, I am eternally thankful.

✦ Natalie Cole

$\mathcal{W}$hen we ask Him for direction, He not only knows what we're saying, but what we *really* mean, where we're coming from, where we're headed — and where we should be headed. We can talk to God often and with absolute frankness, knowing that He always connects with us.

✦ Rachel St. John-Gilbert

Stay Connected

*F*aith is the centerpiece of a connected life. It allows us to live by the grace of invisible strands. It is a belief in a wisdom superior to our own. Faith becomes a teacher in the absence of fact.

✦ Terry Tempest Williams

*W*hen we keep our connections strong with God above, we make our conditions better in the world around us.

As Charles Swindoll reminds us, when you get "things squared away vertically," it helps "clear away the fog horizontally."

✦ Douglas Pagels

You may be experiencing clear sailing right now. Having the all-powerful God as your companion may not seem very important. But I'll guarantee you that your life will not be free of storms — nobody's is. Between today and the day you die, you are going to have your share of heartbreak, disappointment, trial, and tragedy. With God's presence in your life, you will be able to face these storms with confidence.

✦ Bill Hybels

Deep peace of the running wave to you.
Deep peace of the flowing air to you.
Deep peace of the quiet earth to you.
Deep peace of the gentle night to you.
Moon and stars pour their healing light on you.
Deep peace of the Light of the World to you.

✦ Gaelic Blessing

Calm the Waters

$\mathcal{D}$ear God, be good to me.
The sea is so wide and my boat is so small.

✦ Breton Fisherman's Prayer

$\mathcal{W}$e raise the sail of faith. We sail and make this voyage in our little vessel across the turbulent ocean of life. But remember this: No sail has ever moved a ship. *The wind moves the ship.* The sail only catches the wind.

I'm asking you now to raise the sail of faith, and you will capture and harness the power of the spirit of God…. Fresh enthusiasm for life will come like a brisk breeze surging through you.

✦ Robert H. Schuller

There are still many people who haven't experienced the love of God because they don't even know it's available. They don't know God loves them because no one has ever showed His love to them. They would embrace it if they were aware of it, but tragically, they aren't. Imagine a landlocked person who has never seen the ocean. Maybe he's heard about it, but the words he has heard haven't captured it. What would he think when he finally saw it? It would blow his mind, wouldn't it?

✧ Chip Ingram

Some people have never seen an ocean. That doesn't change the ocean. It is constant and powerful, and like the love of God, whether we're immersed in it, standing on the shore, or a thousand miles away, it remains.

✧ Amy Grant

Beautiful Truths

*R*egardless of circumstances and how you feel, hang on to God's unchanging character. Remind yourself what you know to be eternally true about God: He is good, He loves me, He is with me, He knows what I'm going through, He cares, and He has a good plan for my life.

✧ Rick Warren

*M*y familiarity with God's word and my acceptance of His plan for my life kept me from ever really hitting the panic button. In other words, I believe that in reading the Bible a kind of invisible ingredient had seeped into my life — and will seep into anybody's — which makes the rough spots less bumpy....

The Bible takes the scare out of living and puts purpose, joy, and faith in its place.

✧ Dick Van Dyke

Such Wonderful Comfort

When I'm feeling real bad, I put on Aretha Franklin's album *Amazing Grace* and I grab my Bible. I ask myself, "Oprah, are you going to be a victim, or are you going to take charge of your life?" And when I'm in control, I feel like soaring over the mountains. I move with the flow and take life's cures, letting the universe handle the details. I know exactly where I'm going. And God's right beside me all the way.

✦ Oprah Winfrey

The Bible is a penetrating and powerful source of help — it is the wellspring of life. Drink deep while you have the strength. When you are weak, the words will lift your spirit, strengthen your heart, and soothe your soul.

✦ Rachel St. John-Gilbert

The Bible is such a source of strength for me
that it is hard to say which Scripture I look at
for any one thing. But when I feel discouraged,
I read Psalm 23 to restore my soul.

✧ Rosa Parks

The Lord is my shepherd; I shall not want.
He maketh me to lie down in green pastures;
He leadeth me beside the still waters.
He restoreth my soul;
He leadeth me in the paths of righteousness for
His name's sake.
Yea, though I walk through the valley of the
    shadow of death,
I will fear no evil; for Thou art with me;
Thy rod and Thy staff they comfort me.
Thou preparest a table before me in the
presence of mine enemies;
Thou anointest my head with oil; my cup
    runneth over.
Surely goodness and mercy shall follow me
all the days of my life;
And I will dwell in the house of the Lord forever.

✧ Psalm 23 (KJV)

$\mathcal{M}$y times of silence before God are very important to me now. I put everything else down, every word away, and I am with the Lord. When I'm quiet, life falls into perspective for me. I have a very active mind and I'm a worrier, but in those moments when I choose to put that away, I rest beside the Shepherd in still places.

✧ Sheila Walsh

$\mathcal{G}$rant me the ability to be alone; may it be my way every day to go outdoors among the trees and grasses, among all growing things, and there may I be alone, to talk with the one that I belong to.

✧ Author unknown

$\mathcal{G}$od is not in a building, where you can only visit Him on Sunday morning. He is with you everywhere you go.

✧ Joyce Meyer

Don't Miss the Miracle

*L*ord, don't let me take this wonderful gift of life for granted.

What a miracle it is just to wake up in the morning — to be alive another day!...

Remind me to stop sometimes in the midst of it — the often chaotic, maddening midst of it — and touch it, taste it, love it, feel very grateful for it. Let my heart pause to utter a little secret prayer of thanks.

✦ Marjorie Holmes

*I*t doesn't matter how you pray — with your head bowed in silence, or crying out in grief, or dancing. Churches are good for prayer, but so are garages and cars and mountains and showers and dance floors.... As Rumi wrote, "There are hundreds of ways to kneel and kiss the ground." I just talk to God.

✦ Anne Lamott

$\mathcal{A}$ prayer to be said when the world has gotten you down, and you feel rotten, and you're too doggone tired to pray, and you're in a big hurry, and besides, you're mad at everybody... "HELP!"

✧ Author unknown

$\mathcal{W}$hy is it that the bad things in life seem to gang up on us? It can be small annoyances: the alarm doesn't go off, coffee spills on you in the worst place at the worst time, a car won't start. It can be major ones, like dealing with serious illness, financial loss, or death. When a train of negative events or circumstances pulls into our station, we often take it personally. We ask, "Why me?"...

When we're faced with the annoyances or the traumas of life, we need not waste energy trying to place blame or take them personally, as if God is singling us out. What we can do is turn to Him and ask for the peace of mind and strength to rise above.

✧ Rachel St. John-Gilbert

Don't Forget to Count the Blessings

While I'm always ready to ask God "Why me?" when something bad happens, I almost never ask the question when it's something good.

Why me, Lord? Why did I get the gift of a graduate education? Why do I live in a heated, cooled, safe home when so many others don't? Why do I have friends and family who care about me and check up on me when things are tough? Why do I have a reliable car to drive? Why can I go to the supermarket and buy pretty much anything I see there?

If I'm honest with myself, I think I know the reason I never ask God "Why me?" about these situations in my life. Deep down, I believe that I'm the one responsible for all the good things in my life. I have them because I worked hard and so I deserve them. Of course, this is far from the truth....

The bottom line is that all the good things in my life are there because God has given them to me. I need to ask myself *this* kind of "Why me?" much more often.

◆ Karen Stroup

God's faithfulness offers hope for every person, no matter what's going on in your life and how bad it is right now — stress, health problems, financial problems, marital problems, problems with your children, loneliness, desperately wanting to be married, desperately wishing you weren't, or any other issue you might have. Wherever you are and whatever pain you are in, God's loving compassion toward you will never, ever end.

✧ Chip Ingram

My anger about pain has melted mostly for one reason: I have come to know God. He has given me joy and love and happiness and goodness. They have come in unexpected flashes, in the midst of my confused, imperfect world, but they have been enough to convince me that my God is worthy of trust. Knowing Him is worth all enduring.

✧ Philip Yancey

All I Ask...

Lord, you know I've just about had it. Up night after night... and no time to catch up on my rest by the day.

And all the problems. Financial problems, emotional ones.

I feel near the point of exhaustion. Yet I know that if I keep near to you I won't quite collapse.

Thank you for giving me that little extra measure of strength I need to get through each night, each day.

Right now, that's all I ask.

✧ Marjorie Holmes

We can take great comfort that God never sleeps — so we can.

✧ Dianna Booher

Smiles Along with the Tears

$\mathcal{D}$ear Lord,

So far today, God, I've done all right. I haven't gossiped, haven't lost my temper, haven't been greedy, grumpy, nasty, selfish, or overindulgent. I'm really glad about that. But in a few minutes, God, I'm going to get out of bed, and from then on in I'm probably going to need a lot more help. Thank you. Amen.

✧ Author unknown

$\mathcal{W}$hen we believe we are living in God's day, we can experience a sense of relief and humor. We can live this day with joy and look forward to tomorrow with courage and confidence.

✧ Julia Cameron

You have a Father who delights in your laugh, who celebrates your gifts, and who catches every tear that falls from your eyes.

✧ Sheila Walsh

God is the presence, warm, all-enfolding, touching the drab world into brilliance, lifting the sad heart into song, indescribable, beyond understanding, yet by a bird's note, a chord of music, a light at sunset, a sudden movement of rapt insight, a touch of love, making the whole universe a safe home for the soul.

✧ Author unknown

And God smiled again,
And the rainbow appeared,
And curled itself around His shoulder.

✧ James Weldon Johnson

*T*he present chaos in your life and mine is not the final score. We are still in the thick of life. With God's help, we can still salvage this game. We need to keep our heads about us, listen to the coaching, and play our hearts out.

✦ Gracia Burnham

*M*any people fail to obtain the gift of God's power merely because they do not trust their own capacity for faith. They assume they have to be very strong, or truly great saints, but that is not the method Christ teaches. "If thou canst believe," he said, "all things are possible."

✦ Norman Vincent Peale

*F*aith really is amazing. It opens the door for God to get involved in everything we do; and with Him on our team, we cannot lose.

✦ Joyce Meyer

The Game Plan

As a young man, I found a measure of sanctuary and comfort in my faith, a soundproof bunker where I could retreat from pressures. It gave me a way of looking at things and handling them. As I've grown older, I've come to realize that it's more important what you do when you're not in church, but the message of the church is still very valuable to me. When I was playing football, that message insulated me from much of the madness that surrounds a professional athlete. It kept me grounded.

✧ Barry Sanders

I have learned that I must depend on God to do the things I can't do on my own. I used to be so proud of my independence; now I'm grateful for my dependence on God. He gave Brett and me the strength to get through some tough days.

✧ Deanna Favre

I wish I'd known that God would give me all the strength and faith I needed to go through some of my own tough times.... Perhaps I wouldn't have been so afraid.

✧ Maria Shriver

I now know there is a better way. God's way.

✧ Michelle Akers

My heart feels lighter when I consider that God is always available, always concerned, always in control, always competent, always powerful enough to meet my needs.

✧ Dianna Booher

Closer Than Ever

Sometimes I do not feel as close to the Lord as before. I know who has moved. It is not the Lord but Corrie ten Boom. What do I do then? I tell Him who loves me. He forgives and cleanses me and then the fellowship is closer than ever.

✦ Corrie ten Boom

If I get it right I please Him.

If I get it wrong He loves me and gives me another chance.

Because of Him I am filled with joy knowing that I am blessed among men.

✦ Ken Mansfield

What God Is...
and Is Not

God is soft of heart and swift with sympathy toward you. He doesn't hold grudges. His arms aren't crossed. He is not, as I once thought, the cosmic policeman waiting to point out all your felonies and even your misdemeanors. He's cordial, open, friendly, understanding, agreeable, and sensitive to your struggle. Not only that, He longs to express His love, goodness, kindness, and compassion to regular, ordinary people like you and me. God does this not because we have been good or because we deserve it, but because He is good and He wants to. It is part of His very nature and character.

God is divinely and positively disposed toward you. He takes holy pleasure in your happiness. He is not down on you because you live in a fallen world; He is for you in the midst of it.

✧ Chip Ingram

We all need to do our best, work hard, and live wisely, but we must also have faith in God, trusting Him to see us through difficulties, show us how to live, provide for us, and guide us in the affairs of our daily lives....

Yes, we need faith for today and faith for tomorrow. Without this confidence in God, we may be doubtful and hesitant about the present and fearful of the future. God alone gives us strength to face each day, so we need to turn to Him and place our faith in Him alone. Everything else — people, material possessions, education, relationships, corporations, paychecks — may fail us, but God is our Rock, our Refuge, our Hiding Place, our High Tower, our Stronghold in times of trouble, our Secret Place. He is our hope, our peace, our joy, our strength, and the source of everything we need.

✧ Joyce Meyer

The Right Road

As I look back at how far I've come, I realize God has blessed me. And is still blessing me. I am the kind of person who has to literally be knocked over the head to get the point. So through these hard times... God has forced me to open my eyes, examine my life, and find the "narrow road" again. To listen, love, and follow Him. And to trust.

✧ Michelle Akers

Trappist monk Thomas Merton wrote a powerful prayer of faith that speaks to transitions. It begins: "My God, I have no idea where I am going. I do not see the road ahead of me. I cannot know for certain where it will end... [but] I know you will lead me by the right road though I may know nothing about it. Therefore, I will trust you always."

✧ Barbara Bartocci

I can't *prove* that bringing faith into your life will provide you with a gateway to happiness — I just know, based on my own experience, that it can brighten your life in ways you never dreamed. For as long as I've maintained my relationship with God, that gateway has remained open for me. And the profound comfort and happiness I've found on the other side are the greatest gift I've ever received.

✧ Mary Lou Retton

*W*hat we are is God's gift to us.
What we become is our gift to God.

✧ Author unknown

$\mathcal{D}$o you see your God in a fresh light? He is a God who notices and cares about your every attempt, no matter how small, to serve Him. He sees your upturned face, knows your heart, and cares about your faithfulness.

He promises to reward you... and He can't wait to do so!

◇ Bruce Wilkinson

$\mathcal{D}$on't worry about anything; instead, pray about everything. Tell God what you need, and thank Him for all He has done. Then you will experience God's peace, which exceeds anything we can understand.

◇ Philippians 4:6-7 (NLT)

Endless Gratitude

*L*ord, you know how often I mourn for what I don't have: beauty or glamour or brilliance or money. You know how frequently I bewail our family's lacks and imperfections. Please cancel out all those complaints and make a note of this:

Even when I forget to say it, I do thank you day and night in my heart.

✦ Marjorie Holmes

*G*od, you deserve endless gratitude and celebration from all your creation. Thank you. Thank you. Thank you.

✦ Amy Grant

Endless Hope

The final word involves more than life on earth; it involves life in heaven as well.... I find myself thinking often about heaven. Life on earth is real and good.... But life here is not the end. Reality is more than we think it to be. There is another and greater reality that envelops this earthly one.

✧ Gerald L. Sittser

I don't know what tomorrow holds, but that's okay. God does. I don't know what tomorrow holds for you or those who matter to you, but God does. This is not a small piece of information; it is life-changing stuff. Sometimes we have to wait for years for answers. Sometimes we wait a whole lifetime. But trust me... *this ends well for us!*

✧ Sheila Walsh

I don't know the answers, but I know Someone who does.

✦ Author unknown

*G*od's grace has a way of glorifying the past, validating the present, and bringing us into a marvelous future.

✦ Author unknown

*H*e is there, waiting for us to turn our eyes to Him. When we do, we find that He has a better story written for us than any so-called fairy tale we could ever imagine.

✦ Denise Jackson

Acknowledgments continued...

BLUE MOUNTAIN ARTS, INC., P.O. Box 4549, Boulder, Colorado 80306.